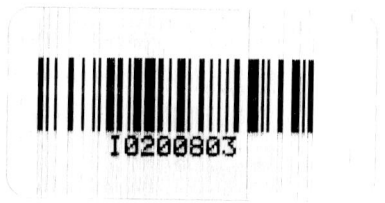

A NEW DAY DAWNS
TAPPING INTO DIVINE SUCCESS

NADINE SMITH

A New Day Dawns: Tapping Into Divine Success
Nadine Smith

Scripture taken from the New King James Version. Copyright © 1982 by Thomas Nelson, Inc. Used by permission. All rights reserved.

Published by
DiViNE Purpose Publishing Self Publishing Platform
www.divinepurposepublishing.com
info@divinepurposepublishing.com

ISBN-13: 978-0692587331
ISBN-10: 0692587330
LCCN: 2015960137

Printed in the United States of America

DEDICATION

I would first like to dedicate this book back to my heavenly Father who has been more to me than anyone else! I am determined that I will always praise you with my life! To my husband and children who have been my biggest earthly strength and support. They made it possible by giving me the time alone when I needed it so that God could speak to me and give divine inspiration.

To my mother, Pastor Velma Smith, who has always recognized and support the gifts and talents that God placed in me. Thanks momma!

To Pastor Andy and Ndidi Osakwe of Summit Bible Church. You have not only given me the keys to become successful in the kingdom of God according to the principles established in God's Word but you have taught me how to walk in and maintain integrity, honesty, and the spirit of excellence. The first half of this book was given to me while under your teaching and I believe that because of such a great beginning, the rest of the book could have a great ending. I love you and bless God for both of you.

To Prophetess Nadine Bowie & Apostle Michelle Kelly. Your passion and fire for the things of God has inspired me to be just as passionate and on fire. You both have become an instrumental part of my destiny and I am blessed to have you both in my life.

To my friend and spiritual sister, Prophetess Michelle McKenzie. You truly are a friend indeed! We've encouraged each other in the most lonely of times and have shared and talked about the dreams and visions God has shown us and have encouraged each other from a place of love and compassion. Thanks for being my friend!

To everyone who has a passion and desire to succeed, remember *Eph. 3:20 (NKJV) Now to Him who is able to do exceedingly abundantly above all that we ask or think, according to the power that works in us.* Know that it is God's power that is at work in you and that *you can do ALL things through Christ who gives you strength. Phil 4:13*

A New Day Dawns for you!

TABLE OF CONTENTS

INTRODUCTION

We've all been given the innate desire for success but many of us still struggle to grasp the ideas and concepts that are rolling around in our minds. Our minds are waiting for us to reach up and out and grab onto those grand ideas and pull them into existence, now, today: at this moment.

Understanding who you are and that you are talented and blessed by God with great ideas and insight into things present and future is the first step on the road to a successful life. Practicality is essential in seeing and manifesting this. No one can experience true success without coming to terms with what's on the inside and bringing practicality to it.

What are you passionate about? What are the visions that you have on the inside? Have you ever looked at a product and thought that you could make it better? Ever woke up in the middle of the night with an idea swimming around inside of you? If the answer is yes, you are reading the right book! If the answer is no, you are reading the right book! Everyone has dreams and visions; everyone has the potential for successful ideas. Some people are just more aware of it than others.

It doesn't matter what stage in life you are in: single, married, rich, poor; busy with kids and school, or even in a state of sadness because of the economic turmoil and conditions all over the world. You can choose right now to be successful. By tapping into your God-given talents and ideas, you can make a new day dawn in your life!

How is this accomplished? Mindset is very important to success! The moment we decide to change our mindset about our circumstances and situation we can be on our way to success. Are you in a terrible situation financially or otherwise? Change your mind set to achieve more. Are you in a situation where you feel financially stable? Change your mind set to go above and beyond that. There is no maximum attainment of success; there is always more to do, more to overcome, more to explore, and more to succeed at. There are too many untapped areas of success for you to just settle with where you are right now.

Vision is an interesting word because it not only refers to what you see in front of you or what you see in five or ten years but what you see for the rest of your life. A vision that expands for the rest of your life is a HUGE vision, but it is attainable. Just dream it and then pray and use the Word of God to speak longevity of life: it is a promised reality!

The Bible says that without a vision the people perish; and that we should write our vision and make it plain for though it tarry it will come to pass. I believe your vision is waiting to burst forth from the inside and "come to pass" as the Bible puts it.

I asked my 13 year old son, Jonathan, today as I was taking him to football practice what makes him get up and go to practice no matter what the weather is like outside and no matter how he feels. He was complaining that his knee hurt and he needed ice. Sometimes someone hits him in the stomach, or he gets hit in his head in the helmet, or his knee is swollen almost twice the size of the other one. Yet, telling him take some time off from football practice to heal is like the worst punishment we could ever give him.

Why is he so determined about football? Because he is passionate about it! He told me that he feels like he was born to play football and I believe him because of all the pain he endures in training and in playing the game and, yet, he goes on every day. Even when he had the flu, he never asked his coach to take him out of the game because he was too sick to play.

Your dream needs passion, determination,

dedication and commitment to what you know is on the inside of you. Never worry about or let failure or trial and error discourage you. No one is ever truly successful on the first try. Success is not about the first try, but it comes at the point where you missed the mark but persisted.

If I ask my kids right now what their plans are for the future, they would be able to tell me. The younger ones draw what they are going to be in the future. Even though some of these goals might be from a child's mind and imaginative as far as being super heroes, they put it on paper. They might not be bitten by a spider in the future and transform to Spiderman, but they are developing the concept of caring for others and might develop community programs with that in mind.

It is important as we go through our lives to not just expect things to happen to us by chance but to tap into that area or areas of success that God has given us and manifest it.

> *Then the Lord answered me and said: "Write the vision And make it plain on tablets, That he may run who reads it."* **Habakkuk 2:2** *(NKJV)*

A group of young kids at my church recently completed their Vision Board projects with awesome results. No two vision boards were the same. Even though they might have parts that relate to another person's vision, it was not an exact match. We are all unique in God's creation of us and in different aspects and angles of life. It doesn't make sense to try to fit into something that is not designed for you. It's like wearing a size 6 or size 10 shoes when you know you are a size 8. The 6 will squeeze you and cause pain while the 10 will fall off and be a nuisance. Only the size 8 will be comfortable and satisfy because it is an exact match. Finding our exact niche will lead us to be passionate and to accomplish what God has designed for us.

While some have tapped into their design, that success that we are called into, there are others who find this difficult. We sometimes struggle with things like self-motivation, confidence, faith, passion and drive, etc. If we follow the Holy Spirit's leading we will be victorious and successful.

I, too, am learning to apply most of the things listed above because I am at the point now where I know that God is saying, "Tap into it, daughter. Tap into that place of success I have called you into." He has given me several areas that must come into play to fully tap into the success which I will be discussing throughout this book.

These are principles and practices, which if followed, will bring forth not only spiritual success but financial success. *3 John 2* *(NKJV)* says *"Beloved, I pray that you may prosper in all things and be in health, just as your soul prospers."* Not only is our spiritual prosperity important to God, but also our financial and physical prosperity. Every area of our lives should be prosperous.

CHAPTER I
DREAM

How important is a dream? How important is it to have something in your mind or in your spirit to hold onto not only today but for your future or for your children's future?

Dreams are why:

- *People invest time, energy and money into projects or people.*

- *Parents work two jobs so the kids can go to school.*

- *My husband and I sacrifice to take our eldest sons to football and basketball practices every day and their games on Saturdays or whenever.*

- *You see, it might not be our dream, but it is their dream and they are good at it. No matter how tired or how much pain our children are in, they never want to miss practice or a game. Our eldest have even broken bones, pulled muscles in various areas of his body and still he refuses to quit! And don't even think about asking them to miss a practice or a game.*

How important is dream? It was so important that a great man, Dr. Martin Luther King, Jr., put it into one of the greatest speeches of all time. Dr. King never experienced his dream, but everything he did was geared towards seeing unity among different races in this country and all over the world. That dream became reality for future generations who were not a part of and probably do not understand the struggles and issues of that time, where color and class clashed, where inequality was the atmosphere of the society and where human beings were classified or viewed in inhumane ways because of the color of their skin.

Even though we still have more work to do, we have made great strides since that speech on August 28, 1963. His dream was for us and our children to experience the unity that God intended for us to have.

How important is dream? It is so important that despite all the bad things that happened to Joseph through the hands of his brothers and through Potiphar's wife, he knew what God had shown him in his dreams *(Genesis 37–48)* We need to understand that just because our dream doesn't line up with our reality, it doesn't mean our dreams will never be realized. Life and it's issues will sometimes cause us to question what God said, and have doubting whether God showed us his plan or did we just imagine things on our own accord. When life looks like it is absolutely heading in the opposite direction of your dreams, like two trains passing by on the tracks, not stopping but slipping away, that's when we have to remember God's word and hold onto his word as good enough to see us through those times of what I like to call "blurred vision."

God is taking His time in fulfilling your dream and there is going to be a spiritual flip, where your dream is realized. That is what happened with Joseph, and he was able to save not only his family, but Egypt and the nation of Israel. Holding onto a dream even when you are experiencing a nightmare will bring breakthrough into your life.

Can you imagine going from the pit to the throne because you held onto something that God spoke to you whether it was twenty years ago, three months ago, or yesterday? Holding onto your dream requires the faith that *Hebrews 11:1* *(NKJV)* talks about: *"Now faith is the substance of things hoped for, the evidence of things not seen."* The substance of your dream is faith and although the evidence is not yet seen, you believe and hold onto that belief with all your heart.

I believe that Abraham's dream must have included having a child in his old age, even though physically his wife, Sarah was past the age of conception. You see, in **Genesis 12**, starting at **verse 1**, Abraham received a promise and a dream from God. Leave everything you know and are familiar with and go somewhere you don't know but I know and I will bless you and make you a great nation. Now with no heir, how can you become a great nation? In order for Abraham to become a great nation, that nation needs to start with his seed, yet his wife had passed that age: Abraham and Sarah were very old.

At the point of Abraham's obedience to God, something was released...The Promise of God became real in his life and over a period of time began to manifest in portions. By the beginning of **Genesis 13**, Abraham was described as very rich in livestock, silver and in gold. This happened as he moved into the vision God had called him to. He held onto the dream that God had promised.

Now imagine this: you were promised,

wealth, blessings, greatness and that in you all the families of the earth would be established. You look at your life and you see that you have already received the wealth, the blessings, and the greatness, so that no one dared to come against you because God was with you. Wouldn't you begin to think about establishing the families of the earth? You certainly would start believing more if God had promised all this and it has happened: He should be able to give seed as He promised.

You see, Abraham didn't laugh because he had no faith and didn't believe, but because he knew that based on all that I've seen you do and fulfill, God, I know it's going to happen and it's going to happen through my old body. I believe he was saying, "Yes, Lord, let it be. Let me enjoy Sarah my wife and bring forth your promise at the same time." The dream must come to pass. God is not a God of empty promises and dead unfulfilled dreams: He is a God of fulfillment, life, destiny, purpose, plans, vision, and He is the ultimate executor of all these things.

"Sarah conceived and bore Abraham a son in his old age, at the set time of which God had spoken to him." **Genesis 21:2 (NKJV)**

Here we have a dream held onto by Abraham and a promise kept by the Lord. The interesting thing about a dream is that you do not have to share it with anyone if you don't choose to. You can hold onto a dream in faith for years until it is fulfilled under God's divine direction and timing. What is the dream that God gave you recently or years ago? Are you still holding on to it in expectation or have cares of life beat upon you so much into the place of hopelessness that you have let go? Well, it's time to pick up that dream, dust it off and hold on to it again in faith because your heavenly father did not change his mind concerning you and that dream he gave you. He is faithful to perform it for you!

Joseph had a choice. He didn't have to share his dreams. It would not have affected the fact that God showed him how his life would be. God protects what He has given us from the devourer. Nothing can separate us from the love of God and nothing can separate us from God's plan for us if we allow God to be the head of our lives. God doesn't give us dreams so that they can be taken away but for them to be fulfilled. In fulfilling your dream the way God showed you, He gets the glory and the praise because you will know that it was not man who did this but God.

CHAPTER II
VISION

"...With man this is impossible, but with God all things are possible." (Matt. 19:26, Gen.18:14)

Did you know our visions can lead us to greatness or lead us to failure? Why is this so? Because our vision can be so great that we either dive in and we see it through to the end and reap the fruits or we become afraid and see how impossible it is to do.

Big visions cause some people to manifest and cause some to hide from it because they just cannot believe because they see themselves as too unworthy, uneducated, or too simple to achieve it. Yes, with man it can be impossible, but with God it is certainly possible!

Vision is so important to manifestation. If you could have a picture of what you're called to do, whether it's kingdom work in the church or owning a business or inventing something new, then you can plan towards it and execute it. If you are in a dark room, looking for something on your table, you can feel around the table and hope that the thing you find is what you are looking for. Or, you can be wise and turn on the lights so that your vision and focus will improve and you can see clearly to reach for exactly what you want. This is how vision works: turn on the lights and don't be afraid to reach for what you want. Vision means actually visualizing not just the initial stages of your dream or idea, but anticipating the manifestation of it; you are able to see your business or idea or invention being successful on the market.

When God speaks to you about your future and all the gifts and talents He has given you to build His kingdom and change lives, He expects you to have faith that it will happen. He expects you to see yourself running that company successfully or working in the ministry effectively, efficiently, and with excellence. *(See Hebrews 11:6)*

The woman with the issue of blood had vision; all she could visualize is touching Jesus' garment. She didn't see the crowd, she didn't pay attention to the people shoving her and complaining that she smelled because of her condition. Her eyes were fixed on Jesus' garment because she could see herself being made whole. That's why she was able to say, *"If only I may touch His garment, I shall be made well." (Matt. 9:21 NKJV)*." Her end result was being made whole, which was her vision.

The Samaritan woman in John 4 not only met a man who told her all she had done wrong, but in order for her to change, she had a vision of all the right things she could do. You can't change someone's life without giving them an alternative way of living; passing from death to life. That's what she saw, a vision of what her life should be and would be.

Vision must be born in the presence of the Lord. You cannot be in the presence of God and leave without your eyes being enlightened. *Ephesians 1:18* puts it this way: *"the eyes of your **understanding being enlightened** (emphasis added); that you may know what is the hope of His calling, what are the riches of the glory of His inheritance in the saints. (NKJV)*

Vision comes from the Master Visionary who knows the beginning from the end. If you have your own vision, please go to God and His Word and make sure that it lines up with His will or ask Him to give you His vision for your life.

Do not accept the lies of the devil in your life. He is a vision stealer and he seeks whom he may devour. God's vision for your life is not contingent upon you being perfect, because as long as you are living in this world you will always be striving for perfection. So if you've made a mistake and strayed away from God's vision for your life, it's not too late to repent and get on the right path with the right vision.

There are many talented musicians and singers who have the right vision from God and have marred that vision with their own plans and have allowed others to lead them away from God's path. Music belongs to God, but sometimes we taint it and God cannot receive that. You'll find that battles were won in the Bible when the singers and musicians were of one mind. When they were placed in the forefront of the army, the children of Israel won the battle.

Some have taken God's vision and given it to the world by playing for the world and singing what the world wants to hear rather than songs that bring pleasure to our heavenly Father. Then, they wonder why they can't succeed or if they find what they think is success, why they are still unhappy? That's because the vision needs to return to God's original intention.

Repentance is returning to God's original intention. He says if we are willing to confess,

He is willing to forgive. Being outside of God's will and intention for your life is definitely a cause for repentance. Many of us are operating that way, but we need to acknowledge and repent. Please take a little time right now to do so.

CHAPTER III
MISSION

"For God so loved the world that He gave His only begotten Son, that whoever believes in Him should not perish but have everlasting life."
John 3:16 (NKJV)

From the beginning, Jesus understood what His mission was and He bore that in mind with everything He did and every trial He faced. I can imagine Him giving Himself pep talks especially in the times when He went off to pray, saying, "Remember the mission, it's not about My will but the Father's will; it's not about Me, but the salvation of the world."

You see, God's dream and vision was to bring humanity back to their rightful position with Him before the fall so we could enjoy all that God has prepared for us from the beginning. Just as He created the Garden of Eden for Adam and Eve's comfort, He was also thinking about us. He realized that we can't make it with just the sacrifice of bulls, rams, and turtledoves offered through the priest once per year.

Jesus' mission was to fulfill God's dream and vision. Your mission is to fulfill your God-given dream and vision. That means carefully planning and executing the mission. Jesus was not confused about why He came as a man and took on sin although He was not a sinner. He knew the mission of redemption had to be fully executed; there was no shortcut or way out and He didn't want one. He prayed in the garden of Gethsemane and ended by saying, *"... nevertheless, not my will, but yours be done."* **Luke 22:42b *(NKJV)***

Realizing that the mission cannot and should not, under any circumstances, be aborted is key to success. It takes determination that has reached the point of believing that the will of God must be done to accomplish this. Mission work is not just writing it on paper but will require action. When you are at the point where you intend to manifest your dreams and visions, you must work at it.

Jesus didn't sit down and wait for the cross to come to Him. He worked up to the point of the cross. He was always out healing the sick, raising the dead, casting out demons, and teaching the poor. He labored every day to bring the vision to pass. Even in times when He felt weak or discouraged, He would go before the Father to get refreshed and then go back out on the mission field. Salvation was His mission, through the cross.

If someone feels called to take the Gospel to Haiti along with food and other necessities, the dream and vision is not accomplished until the mission is completed. If that person stops on their way or decides to turn back, then that mission was not accomplished. Becoming successful will take sacrifice and this is one of the hardest parts for us to accept.

Jacob spent hours one night wrestling the angel of the Lord because his mission was to hang on until he received a blessing. Can you imagine yourself, fleshly and weak, wrestling with and delaying the angel of the living God and living to tell about it? Jacob persevered and even though his hip or leg got disjointed, he was successful in his mission; he received his blessing! *(See Genesis 32:24-30)*

Your journey is just beginning when you come face-to-face with your mission. This is where you use all the strategies and ideas that you received from the Lord. Your mission must come from direction based on what you want to accomplish. You must fellowship and communicate with God to be successful.

It is important to develop a strong prayer life before the Lord, where you learn the presence of Lord and you know the voice of the Lord because your voice and His voice have become one. When you get directions you will know for sure that it is the Lord who has spoken because through prayer and worship you have shut out and rebuked all other voices.

CHAPTER IV
PURPOSE

Many people struggle with this particular word today: **PURPOSE**. Many ask what is my purpose on this job, in this school, in this church, in this family, in this life. What am I to accomplish? Why do I feel the way I do? This all comes down to one thing: purpose. Our lives were meant to be lived with purpose. Since we are called to be purposeful people, anything that takes us away from our mission will cause us to have questions, doubts, fear and stress, and unbelief. Our purpose is to fulfill the mission that God has for us.

Because of growing economic strain and concerns, many people are now forced to examine themselves and their purpose. What is my purpose; why am I here? How can I get to a better place? Our purpose is why we do the things we do.

Many people feel like they are on their own to find their purpose, This can be dangerous because sometimes they end up in places and situations that are really far from the purpose that God as called them to. I have questioned my own purpose many times. Sometimes, I feel like I am walking out my purpose by being heavily involved in ministry. I also have many financially profitable ideas floating around in my head.

There are days when I have more questions than answers about my purpose and destiny and accomplishing them. I have to seek out direction and reaffirmation. The best place for finding what I need has always been in the Word of God. The Bible more accurately defines me than anyone or anything else. When I measure myself through the Bible, I see my purpose.

From a young age, Joseph had visions of his purpose and he kept those visions in his heart and believed that what he dreamt was his purpose. No matter what happened to him, I believe he kept reminding himself of his vision and purpose. When you know who you are and you focus on accomplishing your purpose, then you are able to use every obstacle as a stepping stone. You are able to use issues that arise as building blocks for your purpose. Let's look at Joseph's obstacles, hindrances, and building blocks which led to his purpose:

Obstacle	*Hindrance*	*Building Block*	*Purpose*
Brother's jealousy	Sold into slavery	King's cupbearer	Favor in jail
Unbelief by family	Potiphar's wife	King's baker	Pharaoh's dream

In these times, we must know our purpose and be convinced of it so that we can hold on to it even when we go through rough seasons. Joseph held onto the dreams he received because he believed them and he felt within himself that it is possible. We need to dare to have faith in ourselves and what we can do and we have been called to do. Joseph's purpose was not to serve Potiphar or Pharaoh and to be their slaves for the rest of his life. It was to reach a place of authority in Egypt in preparation for the coming famine so that he could use the wisdom of God to save his family and all around.

Sometimes, it's not just our purpose that brings blessings, but what we do to achieve the purpose will overflow in our lives. Some of us are not even sure what our purpose is, why we are serving the way we are, why we are doing the things we do. We have no ulterior motive, not expecting anything in return, but we serve the ministry, the man or woman of God, and/or our employers faithfully from a genuine heart.

In *2 Kings 4:8-17*, there was a Shunammite woman who knew that there was something special about the man of God, Elisha. She always prepared for him when he was in town. She went as far as to build an extra room on her house just for Elisha because she felt like it, with no ulterior motives. This act of kindness led her to receive a blessing of a son; a child she never had.

CHAPTER V
DRIVE/DESIRE

One of the most admirable traits that you can demonstrate to your employer, friends and family is drive. Drive will keep you going towards your destination. This is the one ingredient to success you do not want to miss. Can you imagine the many items on the market today that took many trial and errors before they became consumer products? It is drive that kept the inventors going. The most successful people (Donald Trump in real estate, Bill Gates in computers, or Henry Ford in vehicle manufacturing, etc.) had to demonstrate and maintain drive to become who they are today. Drive tells you that there is something that you need to achieve and you will not quit until you succeed. Drive allows you to see the diamond in the rough and begin to chisel it out.

According to <u>Wikipedia</u>, WD-40 stands for "Water Displacement – 40th Attempt." In the

Bible, there is a story about a woman whose daughter was being tormented by an evil spirit. This woman knew that she was taking a chance but could not bear one more day of her daughter's misery. She approached Jesus and Jesus' initial reply would have repelled or angered most of us. He told this woman that it was not right to give the children's bread to the dogs. But, this woman had drive; she knew what was important and remained focused. We need to learn not to focus on the negative things that we go through or what people say about us but keep our focus on the goal. Negative events or people may discourage us and diminish our drive, but only if we let them! This woman agreed with Jesus, drew closer to him and worshiped him.

What caused her to do that? Her daughter was at home in need of help. We cannot let offenses and obstacles cause us to abort our mission or lose our drive. We have got to learn to press on, push forth into action despite the trials we face. We are not doing this by ourselves; we have the Spirit of God leading us. The Bible says His path drips with abundance. If we stay on the path and refuse to let anything move us from the way, then we will have the victory and tap into God's success for us. This woman received her daughter's deliverance by persevering and pressing in, never losing the drive to receive her miracle.

Your desire for success will fuel your drive to succeed. What is it that you desire in your life? I believe that everyone desires something. I hope that people desire good things for themselves, their families, and the nations of the world. Whatever your desire, you can bring it to pass with determination.

Desire keeps you up at night creating ideas and products that you know people need. Your desire might not be for a specific business but to be successful in everything you do, which can develop into companies, products and strategies for success. Desire will birth ideas and drive will bring those ideas to pass in your life and in the lives of the people around you.

CHAPTER VI
PASSION

Passion is an interesting topic and the word means different things to different people. Some people equate passion to a sexual desire or feeling that is so overwhelming that it must be fulfilled. While this is true and acceptable within the confines of marriage, passion is reflective of a strong desire which cannot be quenched or fulfilled until it is accomplished. Passion usually has some element or expression of suffering or pain that will lead to purpose.

Passion blinds you from the pain that is usually associated with it. A passionate person often lives in a mindset that even though they are aware of the pain and struggles that might come with reaching their goal; they refuse to be moved by them. The root word for passion is the Greek word *pascho*, which means to *suffer*. When someone is passionate about something, like Jesus was, it usually means that they are willing to suffer loss, grief, pain and anything for that thing or person. Jesus was able to stand the beatings, accusations, scourging, lying, the cross and eventually death for us because he was passionate about us and about reconciling us back to God. *John 3:16* says, *"For God SO loved the world..."* God was so passionate about us and about restoring us that He sent His Son, Jesus, to die for us, to take on our sin and free us from death.

Think about a mother who truly loves her children. She would much rather to be the one suffering or in pain than to watch her children go through it. A mother or father would dash across a busy highway to save their children even though they realize that they may be hit by oncoming traffic. I remember how my husband reacted when he saw our daughter accidentally pushed into a pool by her cousin. He knew she couldn't swim and he not only forgot that he was fully clothed, with his wallet in his pants; he even forgot that he didn't know much about swimming either. The passion for our daughter rose up in him and he dove into the pool and saved her.

Paul, the apostle, suffered much for the kingdom of God yet that did not deter him from his assignment. He suffered much, including being left for dead, but he got up and continued to preach the Gospel. Passion is necessary and makes us willing to suffer pain until we reach our destination. Usually, the things we are most passionate about are the hardest for us to accomplish but that should not hinder us. Pain and suffering build our testimony and helps others who may experience similar situations. Passion places us on the road to destiny and success. It is a necessary ingredient in building character, foundation, structure, wealth, health, relationships and finances.

CHAPTER VII
PLANNING/PLAN

How many times have you been to a seminar and heard the speaker talk about having a strategy for success? I heard this many times at business meetings, in school and even in church.

People once believed that all you needed was a feeling or anointing for something and you could leave it in your head and the Holy Spirit would accomplish it. It didn't work then and I am sure it won't work in today's society. The kingdom of God is a place of order and planning. God expects us to use our gifts and talents and when we plan and execute, we go from glory to glory.

Then the Lord answered me and said: "Write the vision And make it plain on tablets, That he may run who reads it.
Habakkuk 2:2 *(NKJV)*

A written plan enables you to see the necessary steps to accomplish your vision and enlist others, (i.e. workers, volunteers, investors, etc.) to help you fulfill it. Running with the vision means doing whatever is necessary to accomplish it.

Be aware that having a plan does not necessarily mean that there won't be obstacles to overcome. There is no perfect plan and issues may arise. In Acts 6:1, the Hellenistic Jews complained that their widows were being neglected in the daily distribution of food. The Apostles had a plan to reach the nations of the world with the Gospel of Jesus Christ, but this complaint was an obstacle. The Apostles remained focused and decided to make some adjustments by appointing seven men full of the Holy Spirit to oversee this area while they continued in prayer and declared the Word of God. Wisely, the Apostles adjusted the plan a little to include the care of widows. The apostles had to use the wisdom of God to delegate so that the main vision was not compromised and the plan aborted.

CHAPTER VIII
EXECUTION

I wanted to address execution right after planning because I believe that these two go hand in hand. Execution is just as important as careful planning. Even a flawless plan will fail if not executed properly. I call planning the fairy tale stage and execution the reality stage. In the fairy tale stage, everything looks perfect because it's all set in a perfect world with perfect situations and it seems nothing can go wrong. In the reality stage (real world experience) many things may not fit together and can go wrong; that's where execution comes in.

The details of execution must be planned to be successful: how, who, what, why, where must be used in executing the plan. Many of us get stuck in this area. For example, I may get stuck writing this book by doing nothing with it or not knowing where to turn and failing to research how to bring it into the marketplace.

Where do you go to execute? First, you must turn to the One who gave you the plan: God. Seek Him for wisdom and favor in this stage of the plan: prayer and the Word works. Next, know your plan, idea or product. Go over your plan several times with a fine-tooth comb and have others look at it and revise if necessary. It is very unusual to come up with a perfect plan the first time, so you must be open to revising, re-planning, and refocusing. Remember that only God has the perfect plan for your life. Even though He shows it to you, our vision is sometimes tainted by our human nature and this imperfect world.

Developing strategies is important and can be done by simply studying other success stories, after praying. Others have traveled this road before, some have done it several times, and are experts. Ask God for divine intervention and favor and begin to walk it out. You must realize that God's favor is more than money and connections; sometimes it's not who knows you, but who you know. I particularly like this "who you know" aspect because of the implication that even though you are not well known, you know a God who is well known and well able.

In *1 Samuel 30*, David and his men returned to Ziklag and found that everything that they had was taken, including their families, and what was left had been burnt. David didn't lose hope. He just prayed and asked God if he should go get his stuff back. God gave him a resounding yes and David was sure that he already had the victory because of WHO he knew.

My husband, Kes, and I had a plan some time ago. We needed a family van and because we had no finances and no credit, we intended to wait for our tax return and use that to buy the van. We were driving around in a car that had no air conditioning during the summer in Florida. Our three boys were running out of space, especially the eldest who was almost 6 feet tall. He had to sit in the middle because we needed the two youngest to have the only two working seat belts in the car. As soon we received our $4500 tax refund, we planned to head to an auction to buy the van. Unfortunately, this was our first time at an auction and after a long process; we didn't see anything we could afford. Then we saw a Mitsubishi Montero sport which had a third row seat. Before we knew what was going on, we had bid on the vehicle which was $5200 not including tax, title and insurance: great plan, bad execution. While we were nervously waiting, we began to pray and repent.

We acknowledged that we had moved away from the plan and made an error and asked God to show us favor and have them take back the vehicle (in an auction, once you bid and win the bid, you must pay: no changing your mind). We believed God answered our prayer. A few minutes later, the gentleman came and told us that the bank rejected and the bid would not go through.

We laughed and we cried thanking God and returned to the drawing board where we decided on a different route of execution. This time we were successful and we received what we believed God had for us originally. Remember, you must always be willing to make adjustments, not only to the plan, but in the manner in which you execute it.

CHAPTER IX
COMMIT/COMMITMENT

Commitment is an area which is lacking in many people's lives because of the process and strength of will it takes to remain committed. Many people are very committed in the beginning stages of a ministry, a job, a business, or marriage. Unfortunately, when they realize the hard work and dedication it takes to remain; they become slackers and relinquish their first commitment. Sometimes the wrong way just seems like the easiest way to go; being good and upstanding takes too much commitment and resistance.

How many times have you had an idea, project, or new group at work or church that you were very excited about? For the first week or month your commitment level was high. After awhile, you began to lose focus or become bored and attended fewer and fewer of the meetings. Sometimes the thing that distracts us and takes away our commitment is the lack of immediate results or gratification.

In order for your commitment to stand, you must rid yourself of a microwave mentality: if it doesn't happen in a New York minute, we tend to give up. We have to war against that because even though there are instances of instant success, these are extremely rare. Success comes after hard work and commitment to the process.

Marriages fail because people are not willing to stay committed to the vows they took and they aren't willing to work on their marriage. Many marriages end because of abuse, money, or infidelity. The underlying thing is an unwillingness to stay committed to the marriage vows and refrains from abuse, adultery, and stress resulting from using money unwisely.

No individual or company who has enjoyed great success without prolonged dedication. As long as they desired to be successful, they had to stay committed to the vision until they succeeded. No matter how great your plan is, it will not be successful without commitment to the vision. Expect to achieve it no matter what, never backing down, never doubting, and never giving up!

Commitment goes beyond physical strength

and natural abilities. It overrides emotions and desires that are contrary to the vision and it propels you to success. Whether it's a new idea, new invention, a weight loss goal, etc., commitment is vital to your success.

CHAPTER X
DEDICATION/REDEDICATION

My 13 year old son, Jonathan, has a God-given talent in playing the drums. He has never taken a drum lesson in his life, but even before he could walk or talk, I noticed he loved the drums. Whenever the drummer in church started playing, he would raise his index finger from beginning to end. When he got older, he would use every pot, pan, and utensil he could find to make a drum in my mom's kitchen. When he gets real serious and plays the drums, no one compares to him.

Unfortunately, even with all that talent, he doesn't seem as dedicated to the drums as he should be. Sometimes, he plays far below his ability varying his playing style based on his emotions. On the other hand, as I mentioned earlier, he loves football and he is good at it. I believe he was made for football because of his excitement and dedication to the game, notwithstanding the grueling training he endures without complaint. This reflects how dedicated Jonathan is to football.

These two examples illustrate the difference that dedication can make in our life. In the instance of the drums, Jonathan's performance varies by circumstances but in the instance of football, nothing changes his performance. I've watched him play football even when he had the flu.

Your vision and success requires serious dedication and long-term commitment. Even if you have to go to the sidelines to throw up, you must get back in the game and play like the best member of the team. Jonathan has played football with swollen knees, a fractured finger, a sprained wrist and even injuries to his shoulder. He wraps his finger and wrist and puts ice on his knees and shoulders and then returns to the game, even though his mommy is concerned and telling him to stop and rest.

Always remember: "knocked down" does not equal "knocked out." Circumstances and people cause us to feel that we can't make it, and tempt us to take some time off or put that idea on the shelf. I encourage you to get up, wrap your wrist and finger, put ice on your knees and shoulders, whatever it takes, and get back out there. Dedication is remaining committed to what you believe even when others tell you to quit. Commitment is not about your ability to start, but your ability to maintain even in the face of adverse conditions and negative voices.

Remember, your ability to maintain focused and dedicated is not only for you and your success but for your children and their friends, and the world at large. You can leave a legacy of constancy, commitment, and perseverance that is necessary and memorable. Donald Trump or another celebrity's rags to riches story is not the only one worth telling. Your story will only be told if you continue in dedication: *"...be steadfast, immovable, always abounding in the work of the Lord, and knowing that your labor is not in vain in the Lord. (1 Cor. 15:58b, NKJV)*

For those of us who have missed an opportunity to remain dedicated, who failed in the past, it is time to get up, dust off your shelved ideas that God gave you and rededicate yourself to the vision and to your success. Remember what I said earlier: "knocked down" does not equal "knocked out" and that is where rededication comes in. It's not that we missed God or failed that matters. It's that we quit trying. Remember the old saying, "Winners never quit and quitters never win?" We need rededication so we can be winners who never quit.

Returning to the drawing board after a setback can open our eyes to a whole new world of possibilities. We never fail until we give up! If you keep trying and recommitting to the vision, you will eventually be successful.

CHAPTER XI
OVERCOMING ROADBLOCKS TO THE VISION

One of the hindrances on our journey to success and improving ourselves and our lives is **ROADBLOCKS.** No matter what you have determined in your heart to do, whether in the area of ministry, business, finance, or family, you will encounter many roadblocks. It is unwise not to count the cost of this or to ignorantly think that everything is going to go smoothly; absolutely no trouble. Like we say in Jamaica, "No Problem!"

Jesus knew what His purpose was and it was confirmed when He was baptized by John. Jesus prepared himself for his journey. Once, he was led by the Spirit into the wilderness *(the place of nothing in preparation for something)*. He had fasted or **prepared** for forty days when the devil, (ROADBLOCK), showed up. Jesus was not ignorant nor can we be ignorant concerning these things. We certainly cannot afford to get discouraged each time a roadblock occurs.

God has made too many avenues available to us to be moved by one or two roadblocks. So one meeting did not go right: there are ten more meetings to go. So one company or person did not like our idea: there are at least 100 more companies or people who may love your idea and are ready to fund it 100%. Don't forget to use the Word. In **Luke 11:9**, Jesus said, *"So I say to you, ask, and it will be given to you; seek, and you will find; knock, and it will be opened to you."* *(NKJV)*. We can have confidence that whatever we ask according to His will, He hears us.

The devil used three roadblocks on Jesus, tempting him with the lust of the flesh, lust of the eyes, and the pride of life: food, power, and material things. Each time, Jesus used the Word of God to overcome the devil. Notice that the devil also used the Word, but he twisted them. Jesus knew better and spoke the Word, resisting the roadblock and He got the breakthrough!

Here are some simple suggestions for overcoming roadblocks and obstacles to the vision:

ROADBLOCKS TO VISION	WORDS TO OVERCOME
"This is not possible"	I can do all things through Christ who gives me strength
"This is not going to work, just give up!"	Not by might, nor by power but by the Spirit of the Lord
"Sorry, we are not interested at this time"	Ask and it shall be given seek and you shall find, knock and the door will be opened
"I've never seen this work before, how will you make it work"	With man this is impossible but with God all things are possible

OBSTACLES TO VISION	WORDS TO OVERCOME
No money	My God shall supply all I need according to His riches in glory by Christ
No resources	God gives the vision, He will surely give the provision
No human help	And believers were increasingly added... both men and women...
Unsure/doubt/fear	God has not given me the spirit of fear but power, love and a sound mind

CHAPTER XII
FULFILLMENT

Once you have used all the resources available to you and worked hard to bring your vision to pass, you will realize the fulfillment of your vision and succeed. Fulfillment is the excelling moment when all that you have worked for pays off and you finally see your dreams realized.

Many people see this part of the picture even before they see the beginning, the middle, or even the obstacles. At times, when I am involved in a project, I see the whole picture. I don't see it in pieces; I tend to see the final project or the fulfillment of the project more so than the step by step process it takes to get to the final stage.

Fulfillment is a place to rejoice at what has been accomplished and to prepare for what is next to come because it is God's plan and your intention to always strive for more. When one part of your destiny is fulfilled, you move to the next level and the process should continue for the rest of your life. A great example is the evolution of cellphones. Back in 1995, cell phones were so big and bulky that they could not fit in our purses. More people had beepers than cellphones. Today, we cannot only fit cell phones in our purses, but into our pockets. Not only are there are several advancements like Smartphone and iPhone. No more bulk and no more beeper.

CHAPTER XIII
PROMISE KEPT/PROMISE REALIZED

From Genesis to Revelation, the Bible is filled with God's promises for our lives. Because of the integrity of God to keep His promises when we follow his commands, they will always be realized in our lives. As humans, we sometimes make promises that we cannot fulfill and we end up disappointing ourselves and others. I believe that God's abilities have been placed inside us and if we are determined in our hearts and act to see our purpose and destiny through to the end, then we will receive the promise.

God keeps the promises and we get the benefits of realizing them. A promise was given to the Virgin Mary and it was realized in the birth of Jesus Christ whose time on earth was fulfilled by his birth, death, resurrection, and ascension. God's promise to Joseph was kept and Joseph realized the promise which saved nations from a time of famine.

2 Cor. 1:20 says, *"For all the promises of God in Him are Yes, and in Him Amen, to the glory of God through us."* *(NKJV)* It's time to not only receive the promise but keep the promise in our hearts. When God speaks a word to us we must believe by faith in order to receive. What are some of the promises that God has given you since your birth? If they are not fulfilled or realized, it's not because God changed his mind, but either the proper time has not yet come or you have not taken hold of it by faith.

The Bible talks about the seed or the Word being planted on stony ground or good ground and what happens in both cases. When God speaks over your life, the enemy will come to steal that word or cause you to let go of the word and cause it not to mature or bear fruit. Therefore, we must know the strategies to combat the attack of the enemy.

One such strategy is doubt that you are able to accomplish the promise that God gave you. Feelings of insecurity can fuel doubt in your life if you let them. Sometimes our dreams and vision seem so big that we feel that it is impossible to accomplish, especially when we are in a place in our lives when everything is a struggle and we are having serious financial difficulties.

Doubt can only work in your life when you believe that your vision can only be accomplished through your own strength and ability. Doubt feeds on that because when we see how great our vision and promises are, we look at ourselves and decide that it is impossible. Promises are given to you but the ability, resources, grace, and favor to realize them come from God, never from man. *Zech. 4:6* says, *"Not by might nor by power, but by my Spirit,' says the LORD Almighty."* All you need is God's favor upon your life and faith and willingness to allow Him to work it out.

Doubt kills but faith brings life and manifestation. We have to learn to combat doubt with faith. *Hebrews 11:1* states, *"Now faith is the substance of things hoped for, the evidence of things not seen."* Faith must be given the opportunity to work in our lives. Even in the midst of failure, faith perseveres until we succeed. Many great success stories are filled with many failures. When doubt tries to take over, you have got to cancel it, bind it in the name of Jesus, and stand in faith.

Lack is another roadblock that the enemy will try to use against your promise or vision. The devil comes to steal, kill, and destroy and his aim is to show you everything that is lacking. He emphasizes weakness that makes it seem like there is no way you can succeed at this; no way will the promise be realized. But, the devil is a liar! Keep trusting God and remember the word that He spoke to you: He is faithful to fulfill it. For every lie of Satan, God has given us the word of truth to combat it; you just need to be sure that you are using the Word of God.

In today's economy, there is such great lack that many people are even losing their homes. There is no lack or recession in the kingdom of God. The Bible is filled with instances where there was drought and famine but God's people were blessed. God always gives His people divine ideas and strategies in the times of famine that would protect them and make them successful. I believe in this recession, God is giving his people ideas, strategies, concepts, procedures to stand out and to be successful; we just need to tap into it!

What are the divine strategies and ideas God has given you? Begin to run with them. Don't let fear, doubt, or lack discourage or hinder you. Pray for divine direction and favor, believe in faith and follow the instructions that God has given you. There is a company or a group of companies, nations and kingdoms that are waiting for you, your product or service: whatever God has put inside of you. ***Romans***

8:19 says, *"For the earnest expectation of the creation eagerly waits for the revealing of the sons of God."* (NKJV) So go ahead, daughter; go ahead, son: manifest!

CHAPTER XIV
HELPING HANDS

Whatever your vision or product that you want to bring to the marketplace, you are going to need helping hands to bring it to pass. Whether it's friends, family members, your church family, business men and women, you will need others to help you. The first and most important thing to do is bring it before the Lord and ask him to send you the right people and the right opportunity and once you recognize it to take advantage of it.

The Bible is very clear about seedtime and harvest, sowing and reaping. We believe that whatever we sow, we shall reap. So the thing to do is to sow into someone else's life, ideas, vision, or product. My sister-in-law is very good at this. She volunteers a lot and she always puts her best foot forward. Sometimes her volunteering costs money, but she does it with a willing heart and is always available to help others in whatever area she can. She is truly a helping hand to many people, including family, friends and her church. This has caused her to reap many benefits and find favor with many well-known and successful individuals.

I encourage you to volunteer your time in the community as much as you can, doing it with a heart of love because this will open doors for you, not just doors, but the right doors. God uses people and you have to make yourself known so that those people can bless you. Begin to network with different community organizations and events in your area and even outside your locale, if possible. Show yourself to be faithful in serving others, in serving in your church and watch God work on your behalf. God will put you in the right place at the right time to bless you for a long time to come.

Never forget that what you have inside, the talents that God has blessed you with, are never for you alone. I want to say your gifts and talents are for you to serve others with and in doing so you will cause the blessings of the Lord to come upon you and overtake you. When you serve faithfully, God will cause others to begin to serve you faithfully.

You will need people to serve you and to help you with your success, people to mentor you, to encourage you and to run with your vision; you certainly cannot do it by yourself. So even before your vision starts to manifest, begin to invest in others, encourage others, bless them with your presence, pray for them, share ideas, insights and revelations with them. You will not be disappointed when you begin to reap the benefits of sowing into other people's lives.

CHAPTER XV
GIVING THANKS

Phil. 4:6 says, *"Be anxious for nothing, but in everything by prayer and supplication, with thanksgiving, let your requests be made known to God:"* (NKJV)

Many of us miss this important process: the process of thanksgiving. In today's world we only hear "thanks" or "thank you" when something is received. However, we should begin thanking God long before manifestation. In prayer we ask and in the same prayer we give thanks even before we see it because thanksgiving is a faith gesture. It declares that even though we don't see it yet, it is already given and we are thankful that we receive it!

We should live a thankful life at all times and let others know how much we appreciate them by giving thanks for them and to them. Giving thanks shows faith and a heart of gratitude which opens doors. If someone knows that you are the type of person that shows appreciation, then they won't mind helping you whenever you need help. Not only that, but they will be happy to go above and beyond the call of duty just for you.

If you have a problem finding things in your life to be thankful for, just take a walk down the street to the nursing home, the mental health facility, the homeless sites, or just turn your television on and look at the news. You will begin to give God thanks.

I try to have family devotion with my kids every morning and there are some things that we have been praying for many years My youngest, who is now 7, continues to pray for the people of Haiti and his words are always to thank God for healing the people of Haiti. My middle child always thanks God for his family and the oldest always thanks God for protection and helping him to do better.

Giving thanks is not just a onetime thing, but it is a daily thing that should be constant in your life no matter what you do. The more things you see in your life that you know the devil would like you to complain about and be depressed about, the more thanks you ought to give God for because you know that only God can make this better. *1 **John** 5:14* declares, *"Now this is the confidence that we have in Him, that if we ask anything according to His will, He hears us."* Thank him for hearing you and giving you the desires of your heart.

CHAPTER XVI
KEEP GROWING/KEEP MOVING

You must never feel like you have arrived and there is no further to go. The moment you begin to feel this way, you will begin to descend and affect any progress you have made negatively. There is always more to do, more improvement, more glory, more grace, more favor, more blessing.

When Moses sent the twelve spies to spy out the Promised Land, ten came back with a negative report and two, Joshua and Caleb, came back with the report of the Lord; a positive report that they were well able to possess the land. Moses died and Joshua began leading the people. Caleb went to Joshua and demanded the mountain that was promised to him over 45 years before. What struck me is that Caleb declared that he was just as vibrant and strong at 85 as he was at 40. This tells us that Caleb never stopped growing and moving in those years after they conquered the Promised Land.

Never stop moving, growing and reaching for more as long as you are alive because if you do, you will never reach the full potential that God has for you. God requires you to be full and overflowing so that you not only achieve success but you will be able to help others succeed. A glass cannot overflow until it is filled all the way to the top. Once it reaches the top, don't stop pouring, but keep pouring until there is an overflow that will bless others.

Your purpose and vision should determine that you will not leave behind any untapped area of your life, any unfinished task that God has given to you; starting a company, publishing a book, graduating from college with the highest degree does mean that your purpose is over and fulfilled. It just means that this area is complete and it's time to move onto another area or to improve this area.

Caleb could have settled with just living with everyone together in the Promised Land: after all they had achieved it! But, Caleb decided to keep growing and moving, so he requested his mountain so he could start building and constructing a new vision on the mountain that he had inherited years before.

There is no place for retirement in the

kingdom of God so I encourage you to keep growing from glory to glory, strength to strength, vision to vision. Keep moving in the direction of your blessing; keep moving in the direction of your purpose; and keep moving in the direction of your destiny. Remember each day that a new day dawns, is an opportunity to tap into your success!

ABOUT THE AUTHOR

Pastor Nadine Smith was born in the island of Jamaica. She is an ordained pastor, anointed psalmist and worship leader, inspirational speaker, songwriter, author and most importantly, a servant in the kingdom of God.

Pastor Nadine is married to Pastor Kes Smith and they have four beautiful children.

They have a servant's heart toward the Kingdom of God and have been instrumental in setting up and building several ministries in their infancy stage. They recently started Kingdom Builders Christian Center in Houston, Texas, where they are building lives through Kingdom Principles.

Pastor Nadine is available for workshops
and speaking engagements
pastornadinesmith@gmail.com